HOSANNA  MUSIC

Songbook 10

Compiled by Dan Burgess

PRAISE
worship®

FOREWORD

Praise and Worship Songbook Ten includes all of the songs from the following Hosanna! Music albums:

Lord of the Harvest
Men in Worship
Mission of Praise
Rivers of Joy
Shalom Jerusalem
Sing Out

Every song is arranged in four-part harmony (SATB) and can be easily performed by your choir or worship team. The four-part harmony also works well as a basis for piano and organ accompaniment. Cued notes have been added where necessary to help establish the "feel" of the song. Guitar chords are also provided.

Musicians should be encouraged to embellish these arrangements by improvising with the chord symbols. When there is a note under a slash (e.g., F/G), the note above the slash is the chord to be played by the upper register instruments (guitar, right hand of the piano, etc.). The note below the slash is to be played by the lower register instruments (bass guitar, organ pedals, left hand of the piano, etc.). For songs that flow smoothly with each other, a medley reference is listed on each appropriate page.

This songbook has many features to help you plan your worship services.

Index "A" lists all songs by key and tempo. Praise and worship times will flow more smoothly if you select songs that are closely related in key and tempo. Create medleys of songs rather than stopping after each song. Choose songs that are related thematically, such as:

I Will Rejoice	F Major
Shouts of Joy	G Minor
Sing for Joy in the Lord	G Minor
Mourning Into Dancing	G Major

Index "B" lists the songs by topic, such as joy, thanksgiving, victory, etc. If you know the theme of your pastor's message, you can prepare the hearts of the people by focusing your worship on the same topic.

Index "C" lists songs by the first line of lyrics in case you are unsure of the title.

Index "D" lists the songs according to their Scriptural references. If you are searching for a song featuring a specific Scripture, you will find it listed in biblical order.

Index "E" lists copyright owners of the songs presented in this publication.

We wish to thank all those who have given their permission to print the songs in this book. Every effort has been made to locate the copyright owners. If any omissions have occurred, we will make proper corrections in future printings.

TABLE OF CONTENTS

May the words of my mouth and the meditations of my heart be pleasing in Your sight. Psalm 19:14 (NIV)

806 A Man With a Perfect Heart

Words and Music by
JACK HAYFORD

Let me be a man with a per-fect heart,_____ let me be a son who will please You, Fa - ther; Let me be a child who re - veals Your will_____ in all I do and say. Fill me with Your Spir- it, Lord,___ I pray,_____ that Je-sus will be

© 1995 Annamarie Music (Adm. by Maranatha! Music, c/o The Copyright Co., Nashville, TN)
40 Music Square East, Nashville, TN 37203
All rights reserved. International copyright secured. Used by Permission.

Medley options: As for Me and My House; Sanctify My Heart.

If they keep quiet, the stones will cry out. Luke 19:40 (NIV)

807

Ain't Gonna Let No Rock

Words and Music by
DAVID BARONI and
KEVIN SINGLETON

© 1995 Integrity's Hosanna! Music & Integrity's Praise! Music
c/o Integrity Music, Inc., P.O. Box 851622, Mobile, AL 36685-1622
All rights reserved. International copyright secured. Used by Permission.

Medley options: Send It on Down; One of Us; One True Living God.

You, O Lord, reign forever; your throne endures from generation to generation. (NIV) Lamentations 5:19

808　All Around Your Throne

Words and Music by
LYNN DeSHAZO
and ED KERR

All a-round— Your throne,— we come from ev - 'ry lan-guage and— na-tion; Mak-ing Your glo - ries known,— lift-ing a-loud— our song— of sal - va-tion all a-round— Your throne,— all a - round— Your throne.—

© 1995 Integrity's Hosanna! Music
c/o Integrity Music, Inc., P.O. Box 851622, Mobile, AL 36685-1622
All rights reserved. International copyright secured. Used by Permission.

Medley options: I Love to Be in Your Presence; Forever and Ever.

809

All Heaven Declares

Words and Music by
NOEL & TRICIA RICHARDS

1. All heav'n declares the glory of the risen Lord. Who can compare with the beauty of the Lord? Forever He will be
2. I will proclaim the glory of the risen Lord, Who once was slain to reconcile man to God; Forever You will be

© 1977 Kingsway's Thankyou Music/Adm. in North, South and Central America by Integrity's Hosanna! Music c/o Integrity Music, Inc., P.O. Box 851622, Mobile, AL 36685-1622
All rights reserved. International copyright secured. Used by Permission.

the Lamb up-on___ the throne;___
the Lamb up-on___ the throne,___

I glad - ly bow___ my knee___
I glad - ly bow___ my knee___

and wor - ship Him a - lone.
and wor - ship You a - lone.

Medley options: I Stand in Awe; Thank You for the Cross.

810

Almighty

Words and Music by
WAYNE WATSON

© 1990 Material Music (adm. by Word Music) and Word Music (a div. of Word, Inc.)
3319 West End Avenue, Ste. 200, Nashville, TN 37203
All rights reserved. International copyright secured. Used by Permission.

Medley options: King of the Ages; God Is the Strength of My Heart.

I am the bread of life. He who comes to me will never go hungry. John 6:35 (NIV)

811   As Bread that Is Broken

Words and Music by
PAUL BALOCHE and
CLAIRE CLONINGER

1. Man - y hearts are hun - gry to - night,
2. Help us to be - gin where we are,

man - y trapped in dark - ness, yearn for the light; So
help us love the peo - ple near to our hearts; Then

man - y who are far from home and
give our faith a mis - sion field wher -

man - y who are lost, O
ev - er You may call, Lord,

© 1995 Integrity's Hosanna! Music
c/o Integrity Music, Inc., P.O. Box 851622, Mobile, AL 36685-1622
and Juniper Landing Music (adm. by Word Music) and Word Music (a div. of WORD, Inc.)
3319 West End Avenue, Suite 200, Nashville, TN 37203
All rights reserved. International copyright secured. Used by Permission.

pow-er us, Fa - ther,___ to share the love___ of Christ, as

bread that is bro - ken, Lord,_____ use our___ lives.

Medley options: Bread to the Nations; Our Heart.

Baruch Haba
(Blessed Is He Who Comes)

812

Words and Music by
PAUL WILBUR

© 1987 Integrity's Hosanna! Music
c/o Integrity Music, Inc., P.O. Box 851622, Mobile, AL 36685-1622
All rights reserved. International copyright secured. Used by Permission.

Medley options: Ma Tovu; The Song of Moses.

Be It Unto Me

813

Words and Music by
DON MOEN and
CLAIRE CLONINGER

Be it un-to me____ ac-cord-ing to____ Your Word,____ ac-cord-ing to____ Your prom - is-es,____ I can stand____ se-cure; Carve up-on____ my heart____ the truth that sets____ me free,____ ac - cord-ing to____ Your Word,____ O Lord,____

© 1995 Integrity's Hosanna! Music
c/o Integrity Music, Inc., P.O. Box 851622, Mobile, AL 36685-1622
and Juniper Landing Music (a div. of Word Music)/Word Music (a div. of WORD, Inc.)
3319 West End Avenue, Suite 200, Nashville, TN 37203
All rights reserved. International copyright secured. Used by Permission.

Medley options: Lord, I Thirst for You; Like a Shepherd.

814

Blessed be the Lord God of Israel for ever and ever. 1 Chronicles 16:36 (KJV)

Blessed Be the Lord God Almighty

Words and Music by
DAVID BARONI

Lyrics:

1. Thou - sands_____ of thou - sands_____ wor - ship at_____ Your throne,_____ lift - ing_____ our praise to the God of_____ all grace; Your blood has_____ re - deemed_____ us, You've called us Your own._____ To the Lord and to the Lamb,_____ for -

2. Join - ing_____ with an - gels and saints who've gone_____ be - fore,_____ we wor - ship_____ the Lamb, the King of_____ all kings; Cre - a - tion_____ ex - alts_____ You with praise ev - er - more._____ To the glo - ry of Your name,_____ we

© 1995 Integrity's Praise! Music
c/o Integrity Music, Inc., P.O. Box 851622, Mobile, AL 36685-1622
All rights reserved. International copyright secured. Used by Permission.

Medley options: Blessed Be Your Glorious Name; Jesus, We Enthrone You.

He is my loving God and my fortress, my stronghold and my deliverer. Psalm 144:2 (NIV)

Break Through the Chains 815

Words and Music by
GARY McDONALD and
TOMMY WALKER

Break through the chains_____ in my life,_____
tear down the strong - holds and the walls;_____ De -
liv - er_____ me from all bond - age and strife,_____ that
I may hear when You call_____ and give You_____ my

© 1995 Integrity's Hosanna! Music & Integrity's Praise! Music
c/o Integrity Music, Inc., P.O. Box 851622, Mobile, AL 36685-1622
All rights reserved. International copyright secured. Used by Permission.

I sur-ren-der and lay down my life to You, Ho-ly Spir-it, come now and break through. all.

Medley options: He Whom the Son Sets Free; Crown Him.

816 Celebrate the Lord of Love

Words and Music by
PAUL BALOCHE
and ED KERR

© 1995 Integrity's Hosanna! Music
c/o Integrity Music, Inc., P.O. Box 851622, Mobile, AL 36685-1622
All rights reserved. International copyright secured. Used by Permission.

Medley options: God Is Good All the Time; We Rejoice.

Give to the Lord the glory due His name; bring an offering, and come into His courts. Psalm 96:8 (NKJ)

817 Come into This House

Words and Music by
GARY OLIVER

© 1991 Some-O-Dat Music and High Praises Publishing (Adm. by WORD, Inc.)
3319 West End Avenue, Suite 200, Nashville, TN 37203
All rights reserved. International copyright secured. Used by Permission.

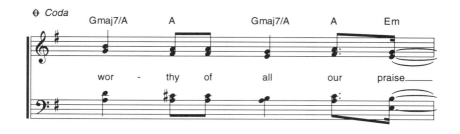

wor - thy   of   all   our   praise._____

Medley options: Hallelujah! Jesus Christ Is Lord; Not by Power.

There is a river whose streams make glad the city of God. Psalm 46:4 (NIV)

818 Come to the River of Life

Words and Music by
DON MOEN and
CLAIRE CLONINGER

CHORUS

♩ = 104

Come to the riv-er of life,___ you will find heal-ing here;___
Come to the riv-er of life,___ come and drink
free-ly here._____ Come if your heart___ is searching, come if your soul___ is thirst-y;

© 1995 Integrity's Hosanna! Music
c/o Integrity Music, Inc., P.O. Box 851622, Mobile, AL 36685-1622
and Juniper Landing Music (a div. of Word Music)/Word Music (a div. of WORD, Inc.)
3319 West End Avenue, Suite 200, Nashville, TN 37203
All rights reserved. International copyright secured. Used by Permission.

Medley options: You Make Me Lie Down in Green Pastures; Pour Out Through Me.

Exalt the Lord our God and worship at his footstool. Psalm 99:5 (NIV)

Exalt the Lord

819

Words and Music by
RICK RIDINGS

Medley options: He Is Here; Blessed Be the Name of the Lord.

© 1977 Scripture in Song, (a div. of Integrity Music, Inc.)
c/o Integrity Music, Inc. P.O. Box 851622, Mobile, AL 36695-1622
All rights reserved. International copyright secured. Used by Permission.

For the Lord is good and his love endures forever. Psalm 100:5 (NIV)

820 For the Lord Is Good

Words and Music by
BILLY FUNK

1. En-ter His gates with thanks-giv-ing,
come in-to His courts with praise;
En-ter His pres-ence re-joic-ing, sing-ing,
"great and might-y is His name."

© 1995 Integrity's Hosanna! Music
c/o Integrity Music, Inc., P.O. Box 851622, Mobile, AL 36685-1622
All rights reserved. International copyright secured. Used by Permission.

Come now__ and bow down__ be - fore Him,_____ lift your

hands in__ praise,__ raise your voice to__ sing.__

For the

Medley options: We Lift Up Your Name; The Lord Be Magnified.

O Lord, our Lord, how majestic is your name in all the earth! You have set your glory above the heavens. (NIV) Psalm 8:1

For Your Glory

821

Words and Music by
SCOTT WESLEY BROWN

VERSE 1

You made the na- tions of the earth, and gave them each a u - nique worth to stand be- fore Your throne, O Lord, and of- fer You their praise; For ev-'ry tribe and kin - dred tongue re-

© 1995 BMG Songs, Inc. (Gospel Division)
8370 Wilshire Blvd., Beverly Hills, CA 90211
All rights reserved. International copyright secured. Used by Permission.

won-ders of Your grace; For ev-'ry na-tion will be healed, and ev-'ry cov - e - nant ful - filled, up - on the glass - y sea, they'll wor - ship Je - sus face to face. For Your

Worship Leader (spoken)
There before me was a great multitude from every nation, tribe, people and language crying out,

Lord.

"Salvation belongs to our God, who sits upon the throne and unto the Lamb, praise and glory, wisdom and thanks, honor and power and strength." Hallelujah!

Medley options: Lord of My Heart; We Are Your Church.

Give and it will be given to you. A good measure, pressed down, shaken together and running over. Luke 6:38 (NIV)

Give to the Lord

822

Words and Music by
RON KENOLY

CHORUS

Give and it will come back to you,___ good meas - ure, pressed down, shak- en to- geth - er and run - ning o - ver; Give and it will come back to you,___ when you give, give to the Lord.___ 1. Give in

2nd time to Coda

© 1995 Integrity's Hosanna! Music
c/o Integrity Music, Inc., P.O. Box 851622, Mobile, AL 36685-1622
All rights reserved. International copyright secured. Used by Permission.

Medley options: For the Lord Is Good; Joyfully, Joyfully.

O great and powerful God, whose name is the Lord Almighty. Jeremiah 32:18 (NIV)

823 Glorious God

Words and Music by
DAVID BARONI, BOB FITTS
PAUL SMITH and CLAIRE CLONINGER

© 1995 Integrity's Praise! Music & Integrity's Hosanna! Music
c/o Integrity Music, Inc., P.O. Box 851622, Mobile, AL 36685-1622
and Juniper Landing Music (a div. of Word Music)/Word Music (a div. of WORD, Inc.)
3319 West End Avenue, Suite 200, Nashville, TN 37203
All rights reserved. International copyright secured. Used by Permission.

Medley options: I Will Rejoice (MOEN); Shout It Loud.

Truly God is good to Israel, to such as are pure in heart. Psalm 73:1 (NKJ)

God Is Good All the Time   824

Words and Music by
DON MOEN and
PAUL OVERSTREET

God is good all the time, He put a song of praise in this heart of mine; God is good all the time, through the dark - est night His light will shine. God is good, God is good all the time.

1. If you're
2. We were

© 1995 Integrity's Hosanna! Music
c/o Integrity Music, Inc., P.O. Box 851622, Mobile, AL 36685-1622
and Scarlet Moon Music (Adm. by Copyright Management, Inc.)
1102 17th Avenue South, Suite 400, Nashville, TN 37212
All rights reserved. International copyright secured. Used by Permission.

good,   He's so   good   all the time.

Medley options: Celebrate the Lord of Love; I Was Glad; Boundless Love.

Surely God is good to Israel, to those who are pure in heart. Psalm 73:1 (NIV)

God Is So Good

825

Author unknown

♩ = 69

1. Di - os bue - no es, Di -
2. De - us é tão bom, De -
3. Ka - ton - da Mu - lun - gi,
4. Mun - gu U mwe - ma,
5. God is so good,

os bue - no es; Que bue - no
us é tão bom; De - us é tão
Ka - ton - da Mu - lun - gi; Ka - ton - da Mu - lun -
Mun - gu U mwe - ma; Mun - gu U mwe -
God is so good; God is so

es, bue - no es el Señ - or.
bom, é tão bom pra mim.
gi, Kat - ton - da wan - ge.
ma, U mwe - ma Kwan - gu.
good, He's so good to me.

Verse 1. Spanish
Verse 2. Portuguese
Verse 3. Lugandan
Verse 4. Swahili
Verse 5. English

Medley option: Joyfully, Joyfully.

Public Domain, This arr. © 1995 Integrity's Hosanna! Music
c/o Integrity Music, Inc., P.O. Box 851622, Mobile, AL 36685-1622
All rights reserved. International copyright secured. Used by Permission.

O Lord, our Lord, how majestic is your name in all the earth! (NIV) Psalm 8:9

826 Great Is Your Name

Words and Music by
JOHN CHISUM

Lyrics:
Great is Your name, O Lord, glo-ri-ous, maj-es-tic in Your right-eous-ness, for-ev-er You're the same; Great is Your name, O Lord, ho-ly and awe-some God, to

© 1995 Integrity's Hosanna! Music
c/o Integrity Music, Inc., P.O. Box 851622, Mobile, AL 36685-1622
All rights reserved. International copyright secured. Used by Permission.

great - er than____ all oth - ers in____ our eyes.____

Medley Options: To the Ends of the Earth; To Thee We Ascribe Glory.

Behold, your God will come with vengeance… he will come and save you. Isaiah 35:4 (KJV)

He Will Come and Save You   827

Words and Music by
BOB FITTS and
GARY SADLER

© 1995 Integrity's Hosanna! Music
c/o Integrity Music, Inc., P.O. Box 851622, Mobile, AL 36685-1622
All rights reserved. International copyright secured. Used by Permission.

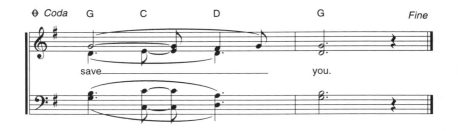

Medley options: I Confess My Trust; Blessed Be the Lord (HAMLIN).

Heal me, O Lord, and I will be healed; save me and I will be saved. Jeremiah 17:14 (NIV)

Heal Me, O Lord

828

Words and Music by
DON MOEN

Medley options: I Will Come to You; Your Steadfast Love.

© 1995 Integrity's Hosanna! Music
c/o Integrity Music, Inc., P.O. Box 851622, Mobile, AL 36685-1622
All rights reserved. International copyright secured. Used by Permission.

829 Heaven and Earth

Words and Music by
LYNN DeSHAZO and
JAMIE HARVILL

© 1995 Integrity's Hosanna! Music & Integrity's Praise! Music
c/o Integrity Music, Inc., P.O. Box 851622, Mobile, AL 36685-1622
All rights reserved. International copyright secured. Used by Permission.

Medley options: You Are Glorious; Lord, You're the One.

Behold, how good and how pleasant it is for brethren to dwell together in unity! Psalm 133:1 (NKJ)

Hinei Ma Tov

830

Traditional folk tune

Public Domain, this arr. © 1995 Integrity's Hosanna! Music
c/o Integrity Music, Inc., P.O. Box 851622, Mobile, AL 36685-1622
All rights reserved. International copyright secured. Used by Permission.

Medley options: Where Does My Help Come From?; Sing unto the Lord.

Holy, holy, holy is the Lord Almighty; the whole earth is full of His glory. Isaiah 6:3 (NIV)

Holy

831

Words and Music by
STEVE TAVANI

Ho - ly, ho - ly Lord, Thou art ho - ly; Please
Purge__ me, cleanse__ me, shine Your light on__ me; And

make__ me ho - ly be - fore_____ Thee.
make__ me ho - ly be - fore_____ Thee.

Medley options: Holy Is Your Name; Worthy, You Are Worthy.

© 1995 Tavani Music/Integrity's Praise! Music
c/o Integrity Music, Inc., P.O. Box 851622, Mobile, AL 36685-1622
All rights reserved. International copyright secured. Used by Permission.

832 Hosanna (Open the Gates)

Words and Music by
CHRIS CHRISTENSEN
and THIERRY OSTRINI

© 1995 Integrity's Hosanna! Music
c/o Integrity Music, Inc., P.O. Box 851622, Mobile, AL 36685-1622
All rights reserved. International copyright secured. Used by Permission.

Medley options: Glory, Glory, Lord; One God.

O Lord, our Lord, how majestic is your name in all the earth. Psalm 8:9 (NIV)

833 How Awesome Is Your Name

Words and Music by
MATTHEW FALLENTINE

© 1995 Integrity's Hosanna! Music
c/o Integrity Music, Inc., P.O. Box 851622, Mobile, AL 36685-1622
All rights reserved. International copyright secured. Used by Permission.

VERSE

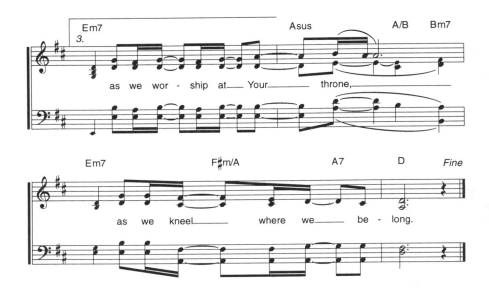

Medley options: I Worship You; We Lift You High.

When God created man, he made him in the likeness of God. Genesis 5:1 (NIV)

I Am a Man

834

Words by
JACK HAYFORD
Music by
JEAN SIBELIUS

1. I am a man, cre - at - ed in God's im - age,
2. I am a man, re - born to serve my Fa - ther,
3. I am a man, ap - point - ed by my Sav - ior,
4. I'll be a man, who walks with God in wor - ship,

of Ad - am's race, now marred by pride and sin.
Your will be done in me, my spir - it cries.
to show His love in all I do and say.
I'll be a man who walks with men as friend.

But through God's Son, Lord Je - sus Christ, my Sav - ior,
My Life has found it's dig - ni - ty and pur - pose,
His Ho - ly Spir - it is my source of pow - er,
I'll be a man, who loves and serves his fam - 'ly;

© 1994 Annamarie Music (Adm. by Maranatha! Music, c/o The Copyright Co., Nashville, TN)
40 Music Square East, Nashville, TN 37203
All rights reserved. International copyright secured. Used by Permission.

Medley options: Pure in Heart; I Was Made to Praise You.

But as for me, I trust in you. Psalm 55:23 (NIV)

I Confess My Trust

835

Words and Music by
PAUL BALOCHE
and ED KERR

I con-fess___ my trust___ in___ You,___ I be-lieve___ You'll see___ me___ through; Through all the hard___ times that___ this life___ may___ bring, I con-fess___ my trust___ in You.___ I con-fess___ my faith___ in___ You,

© 1995 Integrity's Hosanna! Music
c/o Integrity Music, Inc., P.O. Box 851622, Mobile, AL 36685-1622
All rights reserved. International copyright secured. Used by Permission.

Medley options: He Will Come and Save You; You Are My Rock.

836

I Lift Up My Eyes

Words and Music by
ED KERR and
GEORGE SEARCY

© 1995 Integrity's Hosanna! Music & Integrity's Praise! Music
c/o Integrity Music, Inc., P.O. Box 851622, Mobile, AL 36685-1622
All rights reserved. International copyright secured. Used by Permission.

Medley options: Why So Downcast; Lord of All.

I will dwell in the house of the Lord forever. Psalm 23:6 (NIV)

I Want to Be Where You Are   837

Words and Music by
DON MOEN

© 1989 Integrity's Hosanna! Music
c/o Integrity Music, Inc., P.O. Box 851622, Mobile, AL 36685-1622
All rights reserved. International copyright secured. Used by Permission.

Medley options: We Will Meet You There; I Look to You.

But I, by your great mercy, will come into your house;
in reverence will I bow down toward your holy temple. Psalm 5:7 (NIV)

838   I Will Come and Bow Down

Words and Music by
MARTIN J. NYSTROM

© 1984 Integrity's Hosanna! Music
c/o Integrity Music, Inc., P.O. Box 851622, Mobile, AL 36685-1622
All rights reserved. International copyright secured. Used by Permission.

VERSE

Heav- en is Your throne, and the earth is Your foot- stool, Je- sus, I

come to bow down at Your feet. O, how I love just to wor- ship be-

fore You, in Your pres- ence my joy is com - plete._____ So, I will

Medley options: We Dedicate This Time; In Moments Like These.

839

I Will Rejoice

Words and Music by
DON MOEN

© 1995 Integrity's Hosanna! Music
c/o Integrity Music, Inc., P.O. Box 851622, Mobile, AL 36685-1622
All rights reserved. International copyright secured. Used by Permission.

Medley options: Glorious God; Thanks; Why So Downcast?

840

I Worship You

Words and Music by
PAUL BALOCHE
and GARY SADLER

I wor-ship You, I wor-ship You, with ev-'ry-thing with-in me I wor-ship You. For You are the great, most won-der-ful God, wor-thy of glo-ry, rev-'rence and awe; O Lord, I wor-ship

© 1995 Integrity's Hosanna! Music
c/o Integrity Music, Inc., P.O. Box 851622, Mobile, AL 36685-1622
All rights reserved. International copyright secured. Used by Permission.

You,   O— Lord, I wor-ship You.____

VERSE

God of right - eous-ness,____ Lord of ho - li-ness,____

beau - ti-ful____ and per-fect in all Your____ ways;

Ho - ly Lamb____ of God,____ seat-ed on____ the throne,____

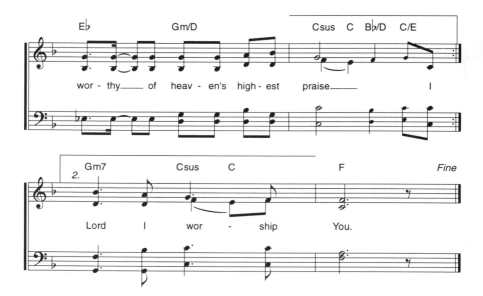

wor - thy___ of heav - en's high - est praise.___ I

Lord I wor - ship You.

Medley options: How Awesome Is Your Name; We Need Your Presence.

You will fill me with joy in your presence. Psalm 16:11 (NIV)

In Your Presence, O God

841

Words and Music by
LYNN DeSHAZO

© 1995 Integrity's Hosanna! Music
c/o Integrity Music, Inc., P.O. Box 851622, Mobile, AL 36685-1622
All rights reserved. International copyright secured. Used by Permission.

Medley options: I Love to Love You; Take Me In.

It is a good thing to give thanks unto the Lord,
and to sing praises unto thy name, O most High. (KJV) Psalm 92:1

It Is a Good Thing

842

Words and Music by
SCOTT WESLEY BROWN
and DAVID HAMPTON

© 1995 Integrity's Hosanna! Music
c/o Integrity Music, Inc., P.O. Box 851622, Mobile, AL 36685-1622
All rights reserved. International copyright secured. Used by Permission.

Medley options: Sing Hallelujah; I Love to Be in Your Presence.

843 Jesus, We Enthrone You

Words and Music by
PAUL KYLE

Je-sus,___ we en-throne___ You,___ we pro-claim You, our
King; Stand-ing here,___ in the midst of us,
we raise You up___ with our praise.___ And as we wor - ship,
build a throne, and as we wor - ship, build a___ throne;

© 1980 Thankyou Music/Adm. in North, South and Central America by Integrity's Hosanna! Music
c/o Integrity Music, Inc., P.O. Box 851622, Mobile, AL 36685-1622
All rights reserved. International copyright secured. Used by Permission.

Medley options: Shout to the Lord; I Sing Praises; The King Is on His Throne.

844 Jesus, You Are So Good

Words and Music by
JAMIE HARVILL

© 1995 Integrity's Praise! Music
c/o Integrity Music, Inc., P.O. Box 851622, Mobile, AL 36685-1622
All rights reserved. International copyright secured. Used by Permission.

Medley options: I Love to Be in Your Presence; Great Is the Lord (CHRISTENSEN).

Sing joyfully to the Lord, you righteous. Psalm 33:1 (NIV)

Joyfully, Joyfully

845

Words and Music by
RON KENOLY

Joy-ful-ly, joy-ful-ly, we are go-ing up,— to ded-i-cate— our hearts— to— the Lord;— Joy-ful-ly, joy-ful-ly, we are go-ing up,— we'll come in-to— His pres-ence— with joy.

© 1995 Integrity's Hosanna! Music
c/o Integrity Music, Inc., P.O. Box 851622, Mobile, AL 36685-1622
All rights reserved. International copyright secured. Used by Permission.

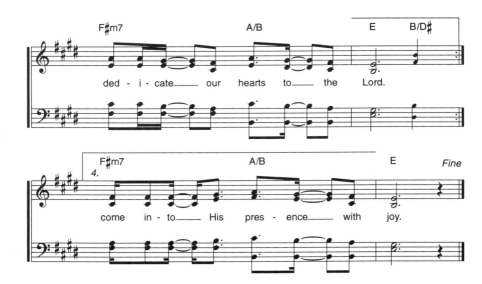

ded - i - cate_____ our hearts to_____ the Lord.

come in - to_____ His pres - ence_____ with joy.

Medley options: My Heart Rejoices; Glory, Glory, Glory.

Fan into flame the gift of God, which is in you. 2 Timothy 1:6 (NIV)

846

Let the Flame Burn Brighter (We'll Walk)

Words and Music by
GRAHAM KENDRICK

VERSE

1. We'll walk the land____ with hearts on fire, and ev'- 'ry
years,____ and still the flame is burn- ing
side,____ one heart, one song, though man- y

step____ will be a prayer; Hope is ris- ing, new day
bright____ a - cross the land; Hearts are wait- ing, long- ing,
streams,____ we'll flow as one; Till Christ's com - pas- sion floods the

calls,____ the King of kings and Lord of

dawn - ing, sound of sing - ing____ fills the
ach - ing for a - wak - 'ning____ once a -
na - tions, and all cre - a - tion____ sees Him

lords,____ faith - ful and true; So let our an - swer re - sound like

thun - der, "Je - sus, Mas - ter,____ we're with

© 1989 Make Way Music/Adm. in North and South America by Integrity's Hosanna! Music
c/o Integrity Music, Inc., P.O. Box 851622, Mobile, AL 36685-1622
All rights reserved. International copyright secured. Used by Permission.

⊕ Coda

shine!_____ Let the flame burn

CHORUS

bright- er in the heart of the dark- ness,_____ turn- ing night_____ to glo- rious

day; Let the song grow loud- er, as our love grows strong- er, let it

shine,_____ let it

shine,_____ let it

Medley options: Shout It Loud; Shine, Jesus, Shine; Stand Up, Stand Up for Jesus.

I will fill this temple with glory, says the Lord of hosts. Haggai 2:7 (NKJ)

(Let Your Glory Fill) This Place 847

Words and Music by
THOMAS D. STERBENS

© 1995 Cantim Music
12936 Sandpoint Court, Ft. Myers, FL 33919
All rights reserved. International copyright secured. Used by Permission.

Medley options: He Is Here; Oh the Glory of Your Presence; Great Is Your Name.

We will shout for joy when you are victorious and will lift up our banners in the name of our God. (NIV) Psalm 20:5

Lift Jesus High

848

Words and Music by
SCOTT WESLEY BROWN

© 1995 Integrity's Hosanna! Music
c/o Integrity Music, Inc., P.O. Box 851622, Mobile, AL 36685-1622
All rights reserved. International copyright secured. Used by Permission.

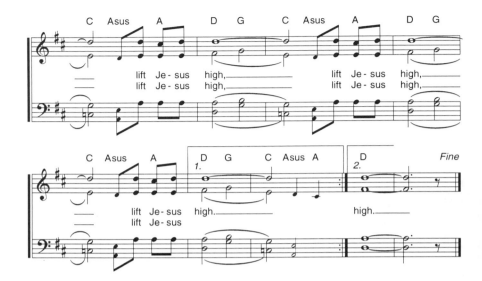

Medley options: Awesome God; He Is the King (SADLER).

Lift up your eyes and look at the fields, for they are already white for harvest! (NKJ) John 4:35

Lift Up Our Eyes

849

Words and Music by
SCOTT WESLEY BROWN

Medley options: Lord, Send Me; Praise to You; Show Us the Ancient Paths.

© 1995 BMG Songs, Inc. (Gospel Division)
8370 Wilshire Blvd., Beverly Hills, CA 90211
All rights reserved. International copyright secured. Used by Permission.

True worshipers will worship the Father in spirit and truth,
for they are the kind of worshipers the Father seeks. John 4:23 (NIV)

850 Live a Life of Worship

Words and Music by
GARY SADLER and
PAUL SMITH

CHORUS

I will live a life___ of wor - ship,___ I will
live a life___ of praise;___ I will lift His name___ a - bove___
all names,___ and high His ban - ner raise.
I will let His Spir - it flow___ through me___

© 1995 Integrity's Hosanna! Music
c/o Integrity Music, Inc., P.O. Box 851622, Mobile, AL 36685-1622
All rights reserved. International copyright secured. Used by Permission.

Medley options: I Was Made to Praise You; In Moments Like These.

Ask the Lord of the harvest, therefore, to send out workers into his harvest field. Matthew 9:38 (NIV)

Lord of the Harvest

851

Words and Music by
JOHN CHISUM and
LYNN DeSHAZO

Lord of the Har - vest,_____ let___ Your voice___ ___ be heard_____ in ev - 'ry na - tion,___ in the far- thest cor - ners of_____ the world;___ Shat-ter the dark- ness,_____ let___ Your truth_____ be known,___

© 1995 Integrity's Hosanna! Music
c/o Integrity Music, Inc., P.O. Box 851622, Mobile, AL 36685-1622
All rights reserved. International copyright secured. Used by Permission.

Medley options: Draw Them Near; Thine Is the Kingdom.

You, O Lord, reign forever; your throne endures from generation to generation. Lamentations 5:19 (NIV)

852 Lord, Take Up Your Holy Throne

Words and Music by
RICK RIDINGS

1. Lord, take up Your ho-ly throne___ deep with-in___ my heart;
2. Lord, take up Your ho-ly throne___ through-out all___ this land;
3. Lord, take up Your ho-ly throne___ through-out all___ the earth;

Take the place that is Yours a-lone,

1. deep with-in___ my heart. And of the
2. through-out all___ this land. And of the
3. through-out all___ the earth. And of the

CHORUS

in-crease of Your gov-ern-ment there shall be no end;

© 1989 Ariose Music (adm. by EMI Christian Music Publishing)
P.O. Box 5085, Brentwood, TN 37024
All rights reserved. International copyright secured. Used by Permission.

Medley options: In the Presence; The King Is on His Throne.

Did I not tell you that if you believed, you would see the glory of God? John 11:40 (NIV)

853　Lord, We Welcome You

Words and Music by
GERRIT GUSTAFSON

We want to see Your glo - ry,——— we want to know Your grace;

——— We want to feel Your pres - ence,———

we want to see Your face.——— We hum- bly bow be- fore———

——— You; We lis- ten for Your voice.———

© 1995 Integrity's Hosanna! Music
c/o Integrity Music, Inc., P.O. Box 851622, Mobile, AL 36685-1622
All rights reserved. International copyright secured. Used by Permission.

Medley options: Come Into the Holy of Holies; Sweet Shalom.

854

Ma Tovu

Traditional folk tune

Public Domain, this arr. © 1995 Integrity's Hosanna! Music
c/o Integrity Music, Inc., P.O. Box 851622, Mobile, AL 36685-1622
All rights reserved. International copyright secured. Used by Permission.

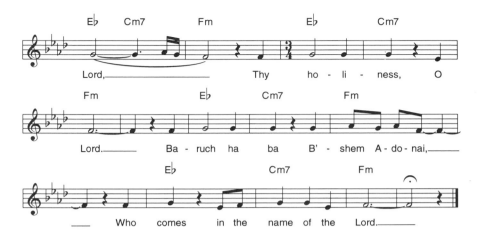

Lord,_____ Thy ho - li - ness, O

Lord._____ Ba - ruch ha ba B' - shem A - do - nai,_____

_____ Who comes in the name of the Lord._____

Medley option: Baruch Haba.

855

Mourning Into Dancing

Words and Music by
TOMMY WALKER

© 1992 Integrity's Praise! Music
c/o Integrity Music, Inc., P.O. Box 851622, Mobile, AL 36685-1622
All rights reserved. International copyright secured. Used by Permission.

F#m7(b5) B7sus D/E   Em7 D/F# G   Am7 G/B C   C/D D   G

I can't stay si - lent, I must sing for His joy has come.
I can't stay si - lent, I must sing for Your joy has come.

1.   G2   2.

Where there

VERSE
G2   C2   G2   Cmaj7 G2/B Am7 Am7/D

once was on - ly__hurt,__   He

G2   C2   G2   C2   G2   C2

gave His heal- ing__ hand;__   Where there once was on - ly__pain,__

Medley options: Lift Up Your Eyes; Blessed Be the Lord (HAMLIN).

Be exalted, O God, above the heavens; let your glory be over all the earth. Psalm 57:11 (NIV)

856 Oh the Glory of Your Presence

Words and Music by
STEVE FRY

© 1983 Birdwing Music (adm. by EMI Christian Music Publishing)/BMG Songs, Inc.
c/o EMI Christian Music Publishing, P.O. Box 5085, Brentwood, TN 37024
All rights reserved. International copyright secured. Used by Permission.

Medley options: I Will Magnify; Lord, Be Glorified; I Stand in Awe.

857

Over All

Words and Music by
BOB FITTS

♩ = 108

O-ver all__ in the heav-ens,__ o-ver all earth-ly do-min-ions;__ O-ver ev-'ry pow'r and prin-ci-pal-i-ty,__ O, Christ rules__ o-ver__ all. O-ver all__ earth-ly na-tions,__ o-ver all the heav-en-ly hosts;__ O-ver

© 1995 Integrity's Hosanna! Music
c/o Integrity Music, Inc., P.O. Box 851622, Mobile, AL 36685-1622
All rights reserved. International copyright secured. Used by Permission.

Medley options: Almighty; King of the Ages.

858 Praise from Every Nation

Words and Music by
GERON DAVIS

© 1995 Integrity's Hosanna! Music/DaviShop
c/o Integrity Music, Inc., P.O. Box 851622, Mobile, AL 36685-1622
All rights reserved. International copyright secured. Used by Permission.

BRIDGE

Medley option: Not by Power.

Let them praise the name of the Lord, for His name alone is exalted. Psalm 148:13 (NIV)

Praise the Name of Jesus, 859
Praise the Son of God

Words and Music by
JACK HAYFORD

Praise the name of Je-sus, praise the Son of God;
Praise the name of Je-sus, praise the Lamb Who died;
Praise the name of Je-sus, praise our ris-en Lord;

Glo-ry, glo-ry be to Christ, our King, Je-sus Christ, Son of
Glo-ry, glo-ry be to Christ, our King, Je-sus Christ, Lamb Who
Glo-ry, glo-ry be to Christ, our King, Je-sus Christ, ris-en

God, Je-sus Christ is the Son of God
died, Je-sus Christ is the Lamb Who died.
Lord, Je-sus Christ is our ris-en Lord.

Medley options: When I Look Into Your Holiness; Victor's Crown.

© 1981 Rocksmith Music, c/o Trust Music Mgt.
P.O. Box 9256, Calabasas, CA 91372
All rights reserved. International copyright secured. Used by Permission.

Rejoice Greatly, O Daughter of Zion! Shout, Daughter of Jerusalem! Zechariah 9:9 (NIV)

860 Roni, Roni, Bat Zion

Words and Music by
DAVID LODEN

© 1977 Integrity's Hosanna! Music
c/o Integrity Music, Inc., P.O. Box 851622, Mobile, AL 36685-1622
All rights reserved. International copyright secured. Used by Permission.

Medley options: Shouts of Joy (UNKNOWN); Sing for Joy in the Lord.

861

Shalom Jerusalem

Words and Music by
PAUL WILBUR

CHORUS

Sha - lom, sha - lom, Je - ru - sa - lem, peace be to you;____ When Mes - si - ah

2nd time to Coda

comes to take us home, may His praise be____ found in you.____

VERSE 1

1. Pray for peace,____ Je - ru - sa - lem,____ cit - y of our God;

© 1987 Integrity's Hosanna! Music
c/o Integrity Music, Inc., P.O. Box 851622, Mobile, AL 36685-1622
All rights reserved. International copyright secured. Used by Permission.

Medley options: Yet Will I Praise Thee; Who Is Like Thee?

862

Shout to the Lord

Words and Music by
DARLENE ZSCHECH

© 1993 Hillsongs Australia
P.O. BOX 1195, Castle Hill, NSW 2154 AUSTRALIA
All rights reserved. International copyright secured. Used by Permission.

_of Your hands,_____ for - ev - er I'll love_____ You, for - ev -

er I'll stand;_____ Noth - ing com - pares_____ to the prom -

ise I have_____ in You._____

VERSE

My Je - sus, my Sav - ior, Lord, there is none_____ like_____ You,_____

_____ all of my days_____ I want to praise_____ the won - ders of Your

Medley options: Jesus, We Enthrone You; Crown Him King of Kings.

Shouts of joy and victory resound in the tents of the righteous. Psalm 118:15 (NIV)

Shouts of Joy

863

Words by
JOANIE MURPHY

This arr. © 1995 Integrity's Hosanna! Music
c/o Integrity Music, Inc., P.O. Box 851622, Mobile, AL 36685-1622
All rights reserved. International copyright secured. Used by Permission.

Medley options: Sing for Joy in the Lord; Roni, Roni, Bat Zion.

864 Sing for Joy in the Lord

Words and Music by
JOHN SELLERS

© 1984 Integrity's Hosanna! Music
c/o Integrity Music, Inc., P.O. Box 851622, Mobile, AL 36685-1622
All rights reserved. International copyright secured. Used by Permission.

Medley options: Shouts of Joy (UNKNOWN); Roni, Roni, Bat Zion.

Sing praises to the Lord, enthroned in Zion; proclaim among the nations what he has done. Psalm 9:11 (NIV)

Sing Hallelujah

865

Words and Music by
PAUL WILBUR

♩ = 104 to 144*

VERSE

Come, let us sing___ for joy___ to the Lord,___ let us shout a-loud___ to the Rock of our sal - va-tion;___ Let us come be - fore Him with thanks - giv-ing,___ and ex-tol Him with mu - sic and with song.___

* At the 144 tempo, the verses
and choruses may be sung simultaneously.

© 1980 Integrity's Hosanna! Music
c/o Integrity Music, Inc., P.O. Box 851622, Mobile, AL 36685-1622
All rights reserved. International copyright secured. Used by Permission.

Medley options: Let Us Adore; Make a Joyful Noise.

Sing out the honor of His name; make His praise glorious. Psalm 66:2 (NKJ)

866

Sing Out

Words and Music by
PAUL BALOCHE
and ED KERR

CHORUS

Sing out, the Lord is near, build Him a tem-ple here; A pal-ace of praise, a throne of thanks-giv-ing, made for the King of kings. Sing out a joy-ful song,

© 1995 Integrity's Hosanna! Music
c/o Integrity Music, Inc., P.O. Box 851622, Mobile, AL 36685-1622
All rights reserved. International copyright secured. Used by Permission.

His love goes on and on; When prais-es a-bound, His

glo - ry sur-rounds us, fill - ing His tem-ple here,

last time to Coda

sing out, the Lord is near. 1. The
2. We

VERSE

Lord in - hab - its the song of His saints and lives in their
come to wor - ship to - geth - er as one, with mu - sic and

prais - es; The Lord in - hab - its the song of His
sing - ing; Re - joice in all that the Fa - ther has

Medley options: What a Refuge; When the Righteous Prosper.

O Lord God Almighty, who is like you? Psalm 89:8 (NIV)

Stand Up and Give Him the Praise

867

Words and Music by
LYNN DeSHAZO

© 1995 Integrity's Hosanna! Music
c/o Integrity Music, Inc., P.O. Box 851622, Mobile, AL 36685-1622
All rights reserved. International copyright secured. Used by Permission.

D.C. al Fine

name of the Lord___ is to be praised.

Medley options: Praise the Lord (GUSTAFSON); Lord of All.

868 The Lord Be Magnified

Words and Music by
BOB AYALA

© 1993 Integrity's Hosanna! Music
c/o Integrity Music, Inc., P.O. Box 851622, Mobile, AL 36685-1622
All rights reserved. International copyright secured. Used by Permission.

O, the Lord,____ O, the Lord;____ O, the Lord be mag-ni - fied.____ O the Lord be mag - ni - fied.____

Medley options: Come to the River; Blessed Be the Lord Almighty.

The People on Your Heart

869

Words and Music by
LYNN DeSHAZO
and GARY SADLER

1. Here I am,___ my Fa - ther,___ wait-ing for___ Your word,___
2. Rul - er of___ the heav - ens,___ Mak-er of___ the earth,___

___ speak, and I___ will hear___ You,___
___ bless - ed Lord___ and Sav - ior,___

show me how___ to serve;___ The man who needs___ Your
bring Your plans___ to birth;___ As I'm in - ter -

mer - cy, the child who's lost___ her___ way,___
ced - ing, Spir - it, light___ my___ way,___

© 1995 Integrity's Hosanna! Music
c/o Integrity Music, Inc., P.O. Box 851622, Mobile, AL 36685-1622
All rights reserved. International copyright secured. Used by Permission.

Medley options: People of All Nations; Heart for the Nations.

This Is the Gospel of Christ   870

Words and Music by
SCOTT WESLEY BROWN

© 1995 Integrity's Hosanna! Music
c/o Integrity Music, Inc., P.O. Box 851622, Mobile, AL 36685-1622
All rights reserved. International copyright secured. Used by Permission.

God be the glo - ry, and to God be the glo-ry; And to God be the glo - - ry, this is the Gos - pel of Christ. And to Christ.

Medley options: We're Not Ashamed; As High as the Heavens.

Like your name, O God, your praise reaches to the ends of the earth;
your right hand is filled with righteousness. (NIV) Psalm 48:10

To the Ends of the Earth

871

Words and Music by
SCOTT WESLEY BROWN
and DAVID HAMPTON

You are ho-ly___ and just, so___ gra-cious___ to us; How___
could we with-hold Your___ praise?___ You are
faith-ful___ and wise, so maj-es-tic,___ O Christ; You are
wor-thy___ to be___ pro-claimed___ To the

© 1995 Integrity's Hosanna! Music
c/o Integrity Music, Inc., P.O. Box 851622, Mobile, AL 36685-1622
All rights reserved. International copyright secured. Used by Permission.

CHORUS

ends of__ the earth You are Lord;_____ From the heav - ens,__ all glo - ry__ is__ Yours._____ We ex - alt You,__ O__ Christ, as we car - ry___ Your__ light to the ends of___ the earth, O___ Lord._____

Medley options: Great Is Your Name; Unto You.

I went up to Jerusalem to worship. Acts 24:11 (NIV)

Up to Jerusalem

872

Words and Music by
PAUL WILBUR

© 1995 Integrity's Hosanna! Music
c/o Integrity Music, Inc., P.O. Box 851622, Mobile, AL 36685-1622
All rights reserved. International copyright secured. Used by Permission.

gates a - gain,____ up____ to Je - ru - sa - lem, up____

____ to Je - ru - sa - lem, up to Je - ru - sa - lem.____

VERSE

1. Je - ru - sa - lem, peace,____ A - do - nai,____ Sar Sha - lom;
2. Cit- y of praise,____ where the tribes____ shout, "Hal - lel"!

Bless- ing be yours,____ God's____ peace with- in Your____ walls.____
We lift our voice____ to the God of Is - ra - el.____

Medley options: One God; Sing and Be Glad in Him.

Yours, O Lord, is the greatness and the power. . . You are exalted as head over all. 1 Chronicles 29:11 (NIV)

We Applaud Your Greatness 873

Words and Music by
RODNEY JOHNSON

© 1995 Refreshing Music
Adm. by Integrity Music, Inc., P.O. Box 851622, Mobile, AL 36685-1622
All rights reserved. International copyright secured. Used by Permission.

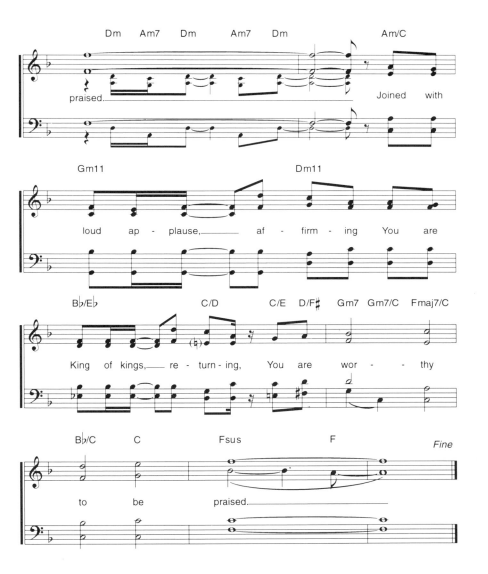

Medley options: We Lift You Up; Lord of My Heart.

Declare his glory among the nations, his marvelous deeds among all peoples. (NIV) Psalm 96:3

874　We Declare Your Name

Words and Music by
PAUL & RITA BALOCHE
and CLAIRE CLONINGER

1. We'll spread the pow - er of Your Word to the
(2. In) ev - 'ry land,___ on ev - 'ry shore, we'll___

far - thest cor - ners of the earth, wher - ev - er there's__ one heart that stands in
tell the world__ Your sto - ry, Lord, un - til the truth__ has bro - ken ev - 'ry

need; We'll speak the name___ that brings the light to the
lie; We'll bring the mer - cy of Your cross to

dark - est cor - ners of the night, to
all the lone - ly and the lost,

© 1995 Integrity's Hosanna! Music
c/o Integrity Music, Inc., P.O. Box 851622, Mobile, AL 36685-1622
& Juniper Landing Music (a div. of Word Music) and Word Music (a div. of WORD, Inc.)
3319 West End Avenue, Suite 200, Nashville, TN 37203
All rights reserved. International copyright secured. Used by Permission.

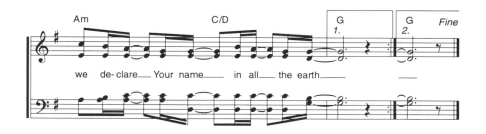

we de-clare___ Your name___ in all___ the earth.___   ___

Medley options: Let Everything That Has Breath; Shine, Jesus, Shine.

875 We Dedicate This Time

Words and Music by
RON KENOLY

We ded-i-cate this time to You,___ O___ Lord;
___ In ev-'ry-thing we say and do,___ be glo-ri-fied.___
___ Pre-cious Je-sus, take Your place up-on the throne of our
hearts; We ded-i-cate this time to You,___ and ev-'ry-thing we

© 1995 Integrity's Hosanna! Music
c/o Integrity Music, Inc., P.O. Box 851622, Mobile, AL 36685-1622
All rights reserved. International copyright secured. Used by Permission.

Medley options: I Will Come and Bow Down; Oh the Glory of Your Presence.

876 ## We Give You Glory

Words and Music by
DON MOEN and
CLAIRE CLONINGER

1. We're here to bless Your name, gath-ered as Your
2. We're here to seek Your face, to gath-er in Your

fam - i - ly; To praise You and pro - claim Your
pres - ence; To cel - e - brate Your grace, to

faith - ful - ness and mer - cy. We give You glo -
praise You for Your bless - ings. We give You glo -

CHORUS

ry, we give You hon - or, we give You ev-

© 1995 Integrity's Hosanna! Music
c/o Integrity Music, Inc., P.O. Box 851622, Mobile, AL 36685-1622
and Juniper Landing Music (a div. of Word Music)/Word Music (a div. of WORD, Inc.)
3319 West End Avenue, Suite 200, Nashville, TN 37203
All rights reserved. International copyright secured. Used by Permission.

Medley options: A Broken Spirit; Unto You (SADLER).

877   We Lift You High

Words and Music by
MATTHEW FALLENTINE
and ROSS PARSLEY

© 1995 Integrity's Hosanna! Music
c/o Integrity Music, Inc., P.O. Box 851622, Mobile, AL 36685-1622
All rights reserved. International copyright secured. Used by Permission.

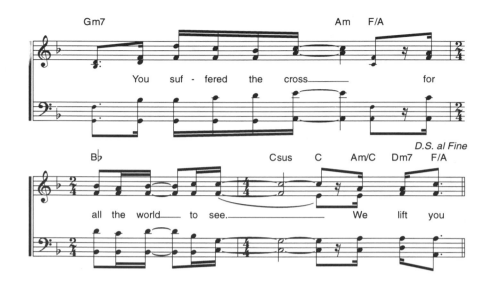

Medley options: How Awesome Is Your Name; High and Lifted Up (SADLER).

Let us draw near to God with a sincere heart in full assurance of faith. Hebrews 10:22 (NIV)

We've Come to Worship You 878

Words and Music by
ED KERR

1. We've heard Your Spir - it call us, in our hearts
2. Hum - bled by all You're giv - ing, we're at rest

You've drawn us near You a - gain,
here liv - ing un - der Your care,

we've come to wor - ship; Leav - ing our cares be - hind us,
we've come to wor - ship; Join - ing the an - gel's cho - rus,

we have faith we'll find Your fa - vor once more,
we sing, "God is for us," morn - ing and night,

© 1995 Integrity's Hosanna! Music
c/o Integrity Music, Inc., P.O. Box 851622, Mobile, AL 36685-1622
All rights reserved. International copyright secured. Used by Permission.

ev - 'ry tribe and ev - 'ry na - - - tion

one day__ will bow,___ we're start - ing now.___

You.__

Medley options: Right Here, Right Now; How Great Is Your Goodness.

879 Where Does My Help Come From?

I lift my eyes to the hills– where does my help come from? Psalm 121:1 (NIV)

Words and Music by
PAUL WILBUR

© 1995 Integrity's Hosanna! Music
c/o Integrity Music, Inc., P.O. Box 851622, Mobile, AL 36685-1622
All rights reserved. International copyright secured. Used by Permission.

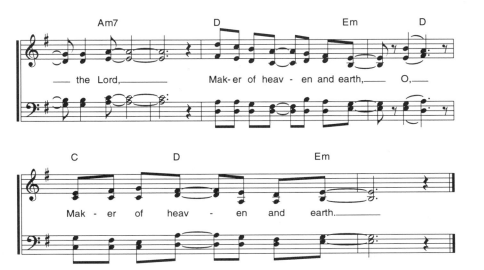

Medley options: Sing and Be Glad in Him; Hinei Ma Tov.

880

With One Voice

Words and Music by
PAUL BALOCHE
and ED KERR

Break out the cym-bals and tam-bou-rines,___

call up the trum-pets and horns;___

Raise up a ban-ner and come with me,___

it's time to wor-ship the Lord.___

© 1995 Integrity's Hosanna! Music
c/o Integrity Music, Inc., P.O. Box 851622, Mobile, AL 36685-1622
All rights reserved. International copyright secured. Used by Permission.

Medley options: Glory, Glory, Lord; We Are Marching.

He will be called Wonderful Counselor, Mighty God, Everlasting Father, Prince of Peace. Isaiah 9:6 (NIV)

Wonderful One

881

Words and Music by
ED KERR and
CLAIRE CLONINGER

© 1995 Integrity's Hosanna! Music
c/o Integrity Music, Inc., P.O. Box 851622, Mobile, AL 36685-1622
and c/o Juniper Landing Music (adm. by Word Music) and Word Music (a div. of WORD, Inc.)
3319 West End Avenue, Suite 200, Nashville, TN 37203
All rights reserved. International copyright secured. Used by Permission.

Medley options: My Trust Is in the Name of the Lord; Give Praise to Jesus.

You made the heavens. . . and all their starry host. . . and the multitudes of heaven worship you. Nehemiah 9:6 (NIV)

882   **Worship You**

Words and Music by
RICK RISO

CHORUS

♩ = 68

Wor - ship___ You,___ I will wor - ship You___ here in this place, I seek Your face and wor-ship You;___ Through all my___ days___ I will give You praise___ Lord, in this

© 1985 Bug and Bear Music, Adm. by LCS Music Group, Inc.
6301 North O'Connor Blvd., Irving, TX 75039
All rights reserved. International copyright secured. Used by Permission.

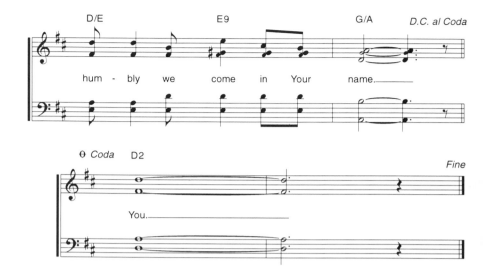

hum - bly we come in Your name._____

You._____

Medley options: I Worship You, Almighty God; Here in Your Presence.

You, O Lord, reign forever; your throne endures from generation to generation. Lamentations 5:19 (NIV)

You Are Glorious 883

Words and Music by
GARY SADLER and
STEVEN V. TAYLOR

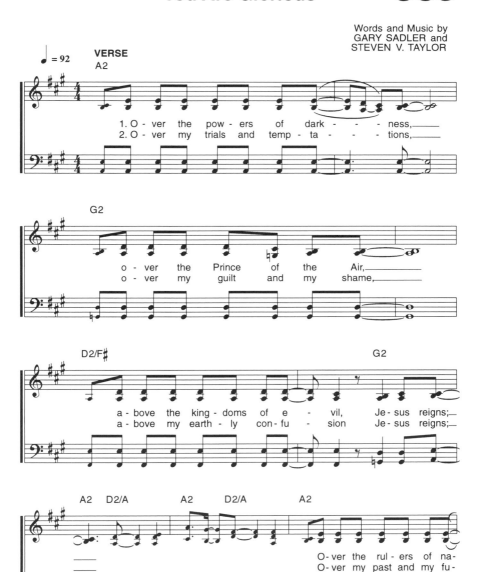

♩ = 92 **VERSE**

1. O - ver the pow - ers of dark - - - ness,____
2. O - ver my trials and temp - ta - - - tions,____

o - ver the Prince of the Air,____
o - ver my guilt and my shame,____

a - bove the king - doms of e - vil, Je - sus reigns;____
a - bove my earth - ly con - fu - sion Je - sus reigns;____

O - ver the rul - ers of na -
O - ver my past and my fu -

© 1995 Integrity's Hosanna! Music
c/o Integrity Music, Inc., P.O. Box 851622, Mobile, AL 36685-1622
All rights reserved. International copyright secured. Used by Permission.

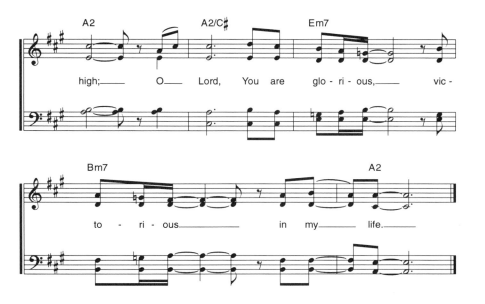

Medley options: Heaven and Earth; We Declare Your Name.

884

You Are Holy

Words and Music by
SCONT WESLEY BROWN

© 1995 Integrity's Hosanna! Music
c/o Integrity Music, Inc., P.O. Box 851622, Mobile, AL 36685-1622
All rights reserved. International copyright secured. Used by Permission.

Medley options: Only Jesus; You Alone Are Holy.

He makes me lie down in green pastures, he leads me beside quiet waters. Psalm 23:2 (NIV)

885

You Make Me Lie Down
in Green Pastures

Words and Music by
KATHY ZUZIAK

Lyrics:
You make me lie____ down in green pas-tures, You make me want - ing for noth-ing, You fill my hun - ger with hon - ey from Your sweet, sweet Word;____ You let me wor - ship be-fore____

© 1985 Integrity's Hosanna! Music/Maranatha! Music
Adm. by Maranatha! Music, c/o The Copyright Co., 40 Music Square East, Nashville, TN 37203
All rights reserved. International copyright secured. Used by Permission.

Medley options: Come to the River of Life; Teach Me Your Ways (GUSTAFSON).

INDEX A
INDEX ACCORDING TO KEY AND TEMPO

D MAJOR
Fast

D MINOR
Fast

E MAJOR
Fast

E MINOR
Moderate

E♭ MAJOR
Moderate

F MAJOR
Fast

Moderate
Slow

F MINOR
Slow

G MAJOR
Fast
Moderate

G MAJOR, Moderate, Cont'd.

G MINOR

Fast

INDEX B
TOPICAL INDEX

CALL TO WORSHIP, Cont'd

COMMITMENT

CONSECRATION

DECLARATION

EVANGELISM

GOD THE FATHER

HEALING

HOLY SPIRIT

JESUS, THE SON

JOY

JOY, Cont'd

PRAISE

TESTIMONY

TESTIMONY, Cont'd

THANKSGIVING

VICTORY

WORD OF GOD

INDEX C
INDEX ACCORDING TO FIRST LINES

INDEX D
INDEX ACCORDING TO SCRIPTURE REFERENCE

INDEX E
INDEX OF COPYRIGHT OWNERS

ANNAMARIE MUSIC, (Adm. by Maranatha! Music, c/o The Copyright Co., Nashville, TN), 40 Music Square East, Nashville, TN 37203: Selections 806, 834.

ARIOSE MUSIC, (adm. by EMI Christian Music Publishing), P.O. Box 5085, Brentwood, TN 37024: Selection 852.

BIRDWING MUSIC, (adm. by EMI Christian Music Publishing), P.O. Box 5085, Brentwood, TN 37024: Selection 856.

BMG SONGS, INC. (GOSPEL DIVISION), 8370 Wilshire Blvd., Beverly Hills, CA 90211: Selections 821, 849, 856.

BUG AND BEAR MUSIC, Adm. by LCS Music Group, Inc., 6301 North O'Connor Blvd., Irving, TX 75039: Selection 882.

CANTIM MUSIC, 12936 Sandpoint Court, Ft. Myers, FL 33919: Selection 847.

DAVISHOP, c/o Integrity Music, Inc., P.O. Box 851622, Mobile, AL 36685-1622: Selection 858.

HIGH PRAISES PUBLISHING, (Adm. by WORD, Inc.), 3319 West End Avenue, Suite 200, Nashville, TN 37203: Selection 817.

HILLSONGS AUSTRALIA, P.O. BOX 1195, Castle Hill, NSW 2154 AUSTRALIA: Selection 862.

INTEGRITY'S HOSANNA! MUSIC, c/o Integrity Music, Inc., P.O. Box 851622, Mobile, AL 36685-1622: Selections 807, 808, 811, 812, 813, 815, 816, 818, 820, 822, 823, 824, 825, 826, 827, 828, 829, 830, 832, 833, 835, 836, 837, 838, 839, 840, 841, 842, 845, 848, 850, 851, 853, 854, 857, 858, 860, 861, 863, 864, 865, 866, 867, 868, 869, 870, 871, 872, 874, 875, 876, 877, 878, 879, 880, 881, 883, 884, 885.

INTEGRITY'S PRAISE! MUSIC, c/o Integrity Music, Inc., P.O. Box 851622, Mobile, AL 36685-1622: Selections 807, 814, 815, 823, 829, 831, 836, 844, 855.

JUNIPER LANDING MUSIC, (a div. of Word Music), 3319 West End Avenue, Suite 200, Nashville, TN 37203: Selections 811, 813, 818, 823, 874, 876, 881.

KINGSWAY'S THANKYOU MUSIC, Adm. in North, South and Central America by Integrity's Hosanna! Music, c/o Integrity Music, Inc., P.O. Box 851622, Mobile, AL 36685-1622: Selection 809.

MAKE WAY MUSIC, Adm. in North and South America by Integrity's Hosanna! Music, c/o Integrity Music, Inc., P.O. Box 851622, Mobile, AL 36685-1622: Selection 846.

MARANATHA! MUSIC, c/o The Copyright Co., 40 Music Square East, Nashville, TN 37203: Selection 885.

MATERIAL MUSIC, Adm. by Word Music (a div. of WORD, Inc.), 3319 West End Avenue, Suite 200, Nashville, TN 37203: Selection 810.

REFRESHING MUSIC, Adm. by Integrity Music, Inc., P.O. Box 851622, Mobile, AL 36685-1622: Selection 873.

ROCKSMITH MUSIC, c/o Trust Music Management, P.O. Box 9256, Calabasas, CA 91372: Selection 859.

SCARLET MOON MUSIC, (Adm. by Copyright Management, Inc.), 1102 17th Avenue South, Suite 400, Nashville, TN 37212: Selection 824.

SCRIPTURE IN SONG, (a div. of Integrity Music, Inc.), c/o Integrity Music, Inc., P.O. Box 851622, Mobile, AL 36695-1622.

SOME-O-DAT MUSIC, (Adm. by WORD, Inc.), 3319 West End Avenue, Suite 200, Nashville, TN 37203: Selection 817.

TAVANI MUSIC, c/o Integrity Music, Inc., P.O. Box 851622, Mobile, AL 36685-1622: Selection 831.

THANKYOU MUSIC, Adm. in North, South and Central America by Integrity's Hosanna! Music, c/o Integrity Music, Inc., P.O. Box 851622, Mobile, AL 36685-1622: Selection 843.

WORD MUSIC, (a div. of WORD, Inc.), 3319 West End Avenue, Suite 200, Nashville, TN 37203: Selections 810, 811, 813, 818, 823, 874, 876, 881.